BUCKS LEGENDS ALPHABET

Words by Robin Feiner

A is for Giannis **A**ntetokounmpo. The Greek Freak's legendary work ethic and athleticism have helped him become one of the greatest Bucks ever. He captured two MVP trophies and earned seven All-Star selections in his first 10 seasons. Teams build walls to stop Giannis. But he broke through to lead the Bucks to the 2021 title.

B is for Junior **B**ridgeman. This legendary super-sub played 10 of his 12 seasons in Milwaukee, providing consistent jump shooting off the bench in the 1970s and '80s. He retired in 1987 with a team-record 711 games played, earning his No. 2 jersey a spot in the rafters.

C is for Dick Cunningham. A tough presence inside and an expert screen setter, Cunningham backed up Kareem Abdul-Jabbar (then Lew Alcindor) in the team's early days. The Cement Mixer's first three-year stint with Milwaukee ended with the legendary 1971 championship before a 1975 lawnmower accident forced his retirement.

D is for Bob **D**andridge. Although he was over-shadowed by The Big O and Kareem, the Bucks don't win the championship in 1971 without this legendary small forward's smooth play and undying determination.
A three-time All-Star with the Bucks from 1969–77, The Greyhound retired top 5 in games played, rebounds, and points for Milwaukee.

E is for **E**ddie Doucette. He was the team's first radio play-by-play announcer. In his 16 years with the team, Doucette became known for his fun announcing style and legendary nicknames. Fans can thank him for The King, The Greyhound, and The Cement Mixer. Bango!

F is for **F**ear the Deer. This legendary Milwaukee motto took over the city during the 2009–10 season when the Bucks made the playoffs after being picked to be one of the league's worst teams. Andrew Bogut anchored a stingy defense, while guards John Salmons and Brandon Jennings fearlessly launched shots.

G is for Glenn Robinson. The No. 1 overall pick in the 1994 Draft, The Big Dog was a legendary scorer for Milwaukee. He left the Bucks in 2002 as the second-leading scorer in team history. The two-time All-Star was pivotal to the team's 2001 Conference Finals run.

H is for Jrue **H**oliday. Many worried the Bucks traded too much for Jrue in 2020. But the point guard's steady play and elite perimeter defense helped put the team over the top to win the 2021 title. His legendary Game 5 alley-oop to Giannis is an all-time Milwaukee hoops moment.

I is for Ersan **I**lyasova.
Love him or hate him,
this Turkish forward played
in 583 games across three
different Bucks stints, good
enough for top 10 in franchise
history. When on his game,
his outside shooting, offensive
rebounding, and charge-
taking were bright spots
during some lean seasons
in the 2000s.

J is for Marques **J**ohnson. Michael Jordan grew up with a poster of Johnson on his wall, showing just how legendary Milwaukee's MJ was. A four-time All-Star in seven Bucks seasons from 1978–84, this scoring machine was a strong all-around player who helped the Bucks make a pair of Eastern Conference Finals in 1983 and 1984.

K is for **K**hris Middleton. His legendary pick-and-roll with Giannis has frustrated teams around the league. Middleton worked hard to become a reliable scorer and solid defender, capable of taking over games when necessary. He was crucial to the 2021 title run and has the most threes in team history.

L is for Lew Alcindor. Before Giannis, the Bucks had Kareem. And before he was Kareem, he was Lew. The NBA's second-leading scorer of all time played his first six seasons in Milwaukee from 1969–75. The legendary center left with three MVPs and a title under his belt.

M is for Jon **M**cGlocklin. His outside shooting seamlessly blended with the skills of The Big O and Lew Alcindor to help Milwaukee win the 1971 title. But Mr. Buck's legend grew on the mic, as he has been calling games on the radio and TV for more than 45 years.

N is for Don Nelson.
The NBA's second-winningest coach, this demanding Nellie Ball architect started building his legendary small ball style in Milwaukee. While the team never broke through to win a championship, the Bucks did make the playoffs in nine of Nelson's 10 full seasons from 1977–87, and he was named Coach of the Year in 1983 and 1985.

O is for **O**scar Robertson. One of the NBA's greatest all-around offensive players, Big O ended his Hall-of-Fame career playing in Milwaukee from 1970–74. The point guard quarterbacked the Bucks to 66 wins and the title in his first season with the team, forming a legendary duo with Kareem (then Lew Alcindor).

P is for **P**aul Pressey. This forward with guard skills was a matchup nightmare. A foundational piece of the legendary Nellie Ball system, Pressey is often considered the first point forward. A Buck from 1982–90, Pressey's long wingspan and ballhandling helped him retire as the franchise leader in assists and second in steals.

Q is for **Q**uinn Buckner. A solid player who did the little things right, Buckner was a legendary thief on the court. A four-time All-Defense Team member, he retired with a franchise-record 1,042 steals across his six seasons from 1976–82. He also sits in the team's top 10 in assists.

R is for Ray Allen.
Behind his legendary stroke,
this shooting guard set
a team threes record during
the 2001–02 season.
Allen's 41 points, including
a personal 17–0 run, in
Game 6 of the 2001 Eastern
Conference Finals is an
all-time Milwaukee moment.
Fans fumed at the eventual
Hall of Famer's 2003 trade.

Ss

S is for **S**idney Moncrief. Moncrief set the defensive tone for the Bucks' success that overlapped with his 1979–89 Milwaukee career. The 1982–83 and 1983–84 Defensive Player of the Year and five-time All-Star could do it all on both ends of the court, going head-to-head with NBA icons.

T is for **T**erry Cummings. After following his dreams to Milwaukee, this power forward was unleashed by coach Don Nelson. Cummings was a two-time All-Star in his initial 1984–89 Bucks stretch. His legendary scoring prowess was built on a smooth, strong style and ability to blow by defenders.

U is for Underdog.
Quickly ascending to cult hero status, Bobby Portis joined Milwaukee in 2020 and helped the Bucks capture their first title in 50 years. Known for his grit, motor, and legendary underdog mentality, fans chant "Bobby! Bobby!" when this crucial sixth man gets down to business on the court.

V is for Vin Baker.
Baker entered the league
in 1993 with a legendary
combination of rim-defending
height and scoring touch.
The big man quickly became
a workhorse, racking up
points and rebounds in
three All-Star seasons with
Milwaukee from 1994–97.
He later returned to the
Bucks as an assistant coach
in 2018.

W is for Brian **W**inters.
A lights-out shooter,
Winters was a two-time
All-Star with the Bucks from
1975–83. Though he was
forced to leave the game at
age 31 due to a back injury,
Winters did enough for his
No. 32 to be retired in
Milwaukee.

X is for **X**avier Munford. Some Bucks fans had high hopes for this high-scoring shooting guard after his impressive performance during the 2017–18 G League season. But his inability to cement a spot in the NBA only highlights the legendary gap between the two leagues.

Y is for **Y**i Jianlin. Milwaukee took this intriguing Chinese forward sixth in the 2007 Draft. Unfortunately, the mystery surrounding him was more memorable than his play. From his legendary rumored pre-Draft workout against a chair to the Bucks having to convince him to come play, Yi was a selection fans still haven't forgotten.

Z is for Bill Zopf.
He was a rookie on the legendary 1970–71 team that won Milwaukee's first NBA title. Zopf got his chance to contribute later in the season, taking injured guard Lucius Allen's spot in the rotation. But Zopf got called up to the Army reserve, missing the championship run.

The ever-expanding legendary library

SPORTS WOMEN LEGENDS ALPHABET

GUITAR LEGENDS ALPHABET

CELTICS LEGENDS ALPHABET

CAR LEGENDS ALPHABET

KNICKS LEGENDS ALPHABET

SUPERHERO LEGEND ALPHABET

BASKETBALL LEGENDS ALPHABET

HOCKEY LEGENDS ALPHABET

LAKERS LEGENDS ALPHABET

FOOTBALL LEGENDS ALPHABET

ROLLING STONES LEGENDS ALPHABET

BULLS LEGENDS ALPHABET

EXPLORE THESE LEGENDARY ALPHABETS & MORE AT WWW.ALPHABETLEGENDS.COM

BUCKS LEGENDS ALPHABET
www.alphabetlegends.com

Published by Alphabet Legends Pty Ltd in 2023
Created by Beck Feiner
Copyright © Alphabet Legends Pty Ltd 2023

Printed and bound in China.

9780645851403

ALPHABET LEGENDS